The Apricot Outlook Of
Katherine Koon Hung Wong

DENNIS W.C. WONG

Copyright © 2019 by Dennis W.C. Wong.

ISBN	Softcover	978-1-949723-53-3
	Hardcover	978-1-950580-77-4
	eBook	978-1-950580-78-1

All rights reserved. No part of this book may be reproduced or transmitted in any form or by any means, electronic or mechanical, including photocopying, recording, or by any information storage and retrieval system without express written permission from the author, except in the case of brief quotations embodied in critical reviews and certain other non-commercial uses permitted by copyright law.

Printed in the United States of America.

To order additional copies of this book, contact:
Bookwhip
1-855-339-3589
www.bookwhip.com

Contents

Illustrations 1

Acknowledgements 4

Introduction 6

I Dreamt 8

Epilogue 14

Addendum 15

My Wedding 44

In Memory 45

Beyond the Apricot Outlook 49

Recent Visit to Honolulu 51

The Missing Link in China 55

Who I Am 59

My Philosophy of Life 64

"My Journey" poem 65

Glossary 66

Chinese Apricot

Illustrations

Calendar February 1928

Birth certificate

Grandpa

Grandma

Mom student ID, 1906

Family photo 1916

Family Photo 1929

Sister Mary's birth certificate

Kaimuki house 1948

Wedding pictures 1948

The first seed 1951

The first fruit 1952

Leaving Honolulu 1958

All Hallow's uniform 1958, Easter 1959

Mom's visit to San Francisco 1959

Moved to Hayward 1960

Renee's 14th, Christmas 1975

Mayrose's letter 1975

China trip itinerary 1982

Zarek's high school graduation 2004

83rd birthday

Parkmont 2011

Family tree

February 1928

Sunday	Monday	Tuesday	Wednesday	Thursday	Friday	Saturday
			1	2	3	4
5	6	7	8	9	10	11
12	13	14	15	16	17	18
19	20	21	22	23	24	25
26	27	28	29			

CERTIFICATE OF LIVE BIRTH

STATE OF HAWAII
DEPARTMENT OF HEALTH

CERTIFICATE NO. **151 1928 - 008501**

DECEASED

CHILD'S NAME
KATHERINE KOON HUNG CHUN

DATE OF BIRTH
February 27, 1928

HOUR OF BIRTH
7:00 PM

SEX
FEMALE

CITY, TOWN OR LOCATION OF BIRTH
HONOLULU

ISLAND OF BIRTH
OAHU

COUNTY OF BIRTH
HONOLULU

MOTHER'S MAIDEN NAME
CHEONG YUCK LIN

MOTHER'S RACE
CHINESE

FATHER'S NAME
CHOCK CHUN

FATHER'S RACE
CHINESE

DATE FILED BY REGISTRAR
March 10, 1928

This copy serves as prima facie evidence of the fact of birth in any court proceeding. [HRS 338-13(b), 338-19]

ANY ALTERATIONS INVALIDATE THIS CERTIFICATE

Acknowledgements

The author wishes to thank his wife, Jocelyn, for her support and patience in his endeavors to pursue completion of this book project.

The author also wishes to thank the following men and women for contributing their ideas, information, and experiences-all of which have been woven into the fabric of this book:

Kathleen Mew Lung Wong Vernon,
Wesley Wai Hong Wong,
Renee Ngit Lung Wong Nasario,
Linda Joyce Yuke Lung Wong Carvallyo,
Kayin Tor Nohea Wong,
Laura Montgomery Yates,
Kimberly Chase- Longus.

And his late father, Clifford Kwei Chong Wong, for encouraging him to go to college

"The way she worded her thoughts was what I thought was interesting."

Kimberly Chase-Longus

"The journey is real, more so when you can relate to someone else's journey."

Laura Montgomery Yates

"Fantastic tribute...nice that you didn't edit her style of speaking."

Niki Munoz

"It is full of priceless memories"

Brandon Wong

"Fantastic information…about her and the family"

Norma P. Wong

"Perfect! Very cool"

Letitia Green

"This book is like a diary and easily understood. So written realistically and not flowered up"

James Chun

Introduction

"The Apricot Outlook" is a revised edition of "Senior Biography of My Mom Katherine Wong Age 77", in 2005. It started out as a term paper for my Psychology class.

This story is presented in my mother's own words from recordings by me in the latter part of her life between 2005 and 2009.

In Chinese artwork, flowers, fruits, and trees represent various aspects of life, and if you know the symbolic meaning of a plant, it will enable you to understand the hidden message. Apricots represent the second month of the traditional calendar and that is when they are in flower. Apricots also represent female elegance; the large seed is ovoid shaped like the eyes of an Oriental beauty.

Once upon a time, on a day long ago, my mother, Katherine Koon Hung (Goon Hung- "outlook apricot") Chun, was born on February 27, 1928 in Honolulu, Hawaii. She lived at 650 Keawe Street, Honolulu, Hawaii.

At times, when she begins to reflect on her past, her thoughts flow into the present. She skips through time and mixes Hawaiian and Cantonese words into her English narration. There is a Glossary at the back of the book.

There are plenty of references to sex which she didn't mind sharing, and she learned what to do at the onset of puberty. Even though many of her family aren't here anymore, she will always remember them the way they used to be. She feels as if she has done what she was put on this earth to do, and now it's time to move on. She realizes that she is gifted in some way but doesn't know who will inherit it.

Despite being hypertensive, diabetic, suffering from a lack of exercise, and feelings of depression, her cognitive abilities do not seem to be affected by any age-related impairment, but in October 1991, she was hospitalized for a nervous breakdown at Kaiser Permanente in Martinez, California.

The effect from her recent stroke had left her with sudden confusion and trouble speaking which can affect behavioral and thought patterns, memory and emotions. Through a better understanding of our families, we acquire an appreciation for their struggles, jealousies, and successes, and we are personally strengthened by their journey.

The Apricot Outlook

I Dreamt

I still remember when I was young. I was three years old. My sister was five years old. She died in my arms, and now I don't know how she looked like. I still remember why she died. Doctors told my mother and my father that it was a childhood sickness that she had that caused her death in my lap. I experienced, after that, when I was older, fourteen years ago, my husband, Clifford, died next to me in bed. We had a king-sized bed, and I still have it. I just changed the mattress. I think that is the reason, as I grew up, the second death occurred in my life.

My mother got five children, all boys, and then she had three girls. She got eight children. We lost three children, two brothers and a sister. My mother's midwife, a long time ago, named me Katherine. My mother and father were so busy. I never had a doll.

I had a Hawaiian-Chinese girl, name Becky, died, poor thing. She was going with a Japanese guy. She died at childbirth when the baby was born. So, I lost her entirely. I had two Japanese friends that I go over and eat sushi and raw fish. The girls, Lily and Dorothy, very seldom come over, but the Japanese family took me in.

My father came with the grand uncle. We called him Sook Goong, because he was close to me than my own father's father. My father, a handsome man, died at 65. I didn't have too much of a life with him. When I was nine or ten, I worked at the family laundry business. My dad bought an existing laundry business in Kakaako. It had a kitchen, checking room, bathroom, ironing room, office, and one bedroom for my parents, two sisters and I. All five of my brothers slept in the living room.

The elementary school was across my father's business. I went to Kawanakoa Intermediate School on Nuuanu Street. It was too far away. I had to go downhill; but coming back home, I came on the bus. I don't want to go uphill.

I fold the stockings. I fold the socks, handkerchief. We had to pile them up to go to the mongo, the iron shift, just like how you press the shirts, the pants. My granduncle usually treat me cookies, candies, ice cream. We would buy potatoes, have baked potatoes, marshmallows, and hot dogs. We eat. We get hungry fast because we eat at 4:00. So, at 3:30, the men eat first then us ladies and children eat in the afternoon. At 7:00, we have breakfast. I get donuts. I get bread and jelly. That's all we give the men. At lunch time, we get cold cuts and strawberry again, and dinner time we get rice again. We eat well.

I went out look for dates. You can hear them drop, ripe already. I bring them home, wash it, and eat. We had tangerine. We raised a dog and a cat for the mice. They eat together. I feed them every night and cut some wood for the cooks. We had pigeons. We make food out of them. I was going to make message, put notes, and try to see how you send it out. I tried to do something with the pigeons.

The man came over, got hired for being a cook. He makes good food for us. We all eat so we never go hungry. We have my father, a manager. He's a smart man. He reads the newspaper and listens to radio program. That's how he learned and talking to us too. You guys should know your grandpa, a good looking man and respectful. He makes out the laundry, the bill. My brothers didn't want to take over the laundry business.

We had one dryer. All the clothes came out in the wash. We wash in a big tumbling washing machine. Got hot water coming out for the clothes, as hot as we can take it. We don't want to burn. We bathed in the washroom. We were naked, and we hid behind the laundry. My brothers all go and bathe together. We had hot water in a big tub. We had to cut lumber for the wood, put cold water, and bathe like that and put the soap, rinse, and all pau.

We learn that I was a young lady already. They don't touch me. I learn to get rid of all the blood, rinse it out, and throw it into the family washer when I change my mother's bathing things, bed sheets. Then I get my brother's bed sheets. I help them too. I didn't do it every week, every other week. It's ok. After all we were not really dirty. We take a bath every night, but hard life too.

We get all the sheets, their clothes and put them in our group with my father's shirts, pants, stockings, handkerchief. We wash the family load. The bundles were so high, so heavy. I manage to carry.

My youngest aunty, Betty's mother, took my mother to go shopping. Then my mother got money. She saved too, and whatever my father saved, went and bought the house for us. My mother had the house already picked. So, one day, they engineered, made the pattern of the house. We had three bedrooms, kitchen, and another small prayer room. She goes and cleans the yard. Sometimes she mops the kitchen. People come and get the laundry.

I had my aunties that stayed with us. My life goes out to them because they were good cooks. I learned a lot of things from my aunties, my mother's sisters. I still enjoy cooking. I cook oxtail, Chinese stew.

We lost the business when there was a fire, a short circuit in the washroom. Even the date tree caught fire. My father didn't pay the insurance. We went bankrupt. There was no more job. I wanted to help my folks with food money. My father didn't have too much money already. We lost the insurance. He was in the hole, but I managed, and my brothers tried to help out too, but they just were helpless too.

After we lost the business, my mom had to go to work. She got a ride to work at the naval shipyard during Pearl Harbor attack taking care of the military personnel's children.

I took homemaking and swimming classes at McKinley High School and graduated in June 1946. I learned how to cook. I swim across the pool. I held on to a long stick and swim across the pool. I passed. I wanted to be a beauty operator or a dietician but didn't have the money or the education.

I had a good life. I didn't have the knowledge to be smart girl to go to college. I didn't know what to do. It's ok.

I had a beauty operator across the street introduce me to Lily Wong, a Beautician. She knew how to do permanents. She paid me $1.50 to learn beauty shop. I go there. I shampoo, set the hair, and put under the dryer. I clean up, and

I know how to close the beauty shop. Next weekend, I would help open the beauty shop. I would do a good job. She would give me free lunch too, good lunch.

I didn't know that I met my cousin (Jimmy Wong). He didn't know we were cousins until he told me about his mother and twin sister and my mother's sister too. He was fond of me. I have, in my mind of Clifford, when one of his friends told him Cliff, you have a date. Don't forget. He's going to come and pick you up. So, he came and I met my cousin. He was a driver of my date, and then I met Cliff, my husband, for dinner and dance, and I know he was it. My cousin liked me. I told my parents he was their nephew. I cannot marry him. I kind of liked him too, but Clifford was it.

Dad did join and was admitted to the armed forces for two years. He came back, and he asked me to get engaged, so, he went to the Commissary, and I chose my ring in '47. We got married in '48. I got my jade ring from my aunty, the second aunty. The big aunty gave me the Chinese robe. The jacket, I got from my other aunty. It didn't fit me after I grew and got older.

Dad wanted a Hawaiian Luau. He had friends that who make Luau. So, I had a Luau party. Lot of crashers came in. I didn't care, but my husband put up a lot of money for his friends and to help us for the imu, the pig. We had a good time. My dad wanted a Chinese wedding to show me off to his Chinese club, all high tune millionaire people. He had joined and was accepted into the club.

The grand folks (Clifford's parents) wanted to live where they are. They sold the house in Kapahulu to help us. We went in to buy one home. We saw the place. Dad didn't have enough money to buy a home. We owe Goong Goong $2,000, and Rodney owe about $2,000 too. So, we had three houses in a row.

Rodney was going to get married right after us. Then Aunty Jessie came home and got married. She was pregnant right away because she was old. Mayrose was pregnant on the following year. So, all gave birth. I was jealous because they got children. I didn't want to wait too long. So, I want children to grow up with the sister's children. He hold back on me because he wanted to own the house. You can't own the house overnight, I said you stupid, dumb. You don't think that way. I told Cliff why shouldn't we have children too so they grow up together. So, he finally considered that, and I got pregnant on you. I had a hard time because of my back. I worked too early.

We slept in the same bed, but I knew everything about sex. I kind of know. I do some reading too. We had our own room, and when you were born, you would go in the big room. We took the second room. Goong Goong would help us build that section. It was L-shaped. He fixed it up for us. Then Kathy was born, and Debbie was born, and Wesley was born. So, we had four children together.

The big bedroom, with the stairs that go down, is where uncle Bill stayed on the double bed. I had a double bed.

Aunty Lily opened her mouth. Oh, why can't you folks? You have an extra room. Why shouldn't you have uncle Bill stay with you? He didn't give me anything until after a while, he noticed that I've been paying water bill and gas bill and all that. The money we had to pay back grandpa what we borrowed. I didn't like the idea that Aunty Lily opened her mouth, and that he stayed. He cleaned the room. He cleans the bathroom. All clean.

After I got married, I worked at the controller's office. I type the figures of what we make for the company at Alexander Young Hotel, a VonHamm Young company. I didn't get good pay. The money was ok, but I didn't want to quit work and go get another job. Daddy said go ahead even though it would help us with food money. I did work until I got pregnant.

They had a bakery on the side. I love the pastries over there. I buy donuts, pastries, cinnamon roll, cupcakes. At the laundry business, I get 50% off. I send Goong Goong's shirts and sheets. I told the grandmother don't wash the sheets. Send them out because I get discount. I've been paying for that. I worked at National Department store in Honolulu. I was the sales girl.

My father was sick. He couldn't walk. He was bedridden. He had a heart attack and died at 65 (March 1953).

I was going to call you Daniel, or David, or something like that, but I told dad how about Dennis? He said up to you. I said ok, Dennis. Then Goong Goong chose your name Wai Chung, Wai Hong for Wesley. Then the girls all Lung, Lung, Lung, Lung. I love Kathleen. Pretty Kathleen song, I sang. How about Deborah, nickname Debbie. She's a peanut one. Deborah was the smallest in weight (6 lb. 8-3/4 oz). I had to take care of myself.

I had a Portuguese woman that my mother found and called her saying that she's going to bring her daughter to come over and massage the baby to bring her in the right position. So, she was leg, head down. I had a normal birth after that. With Wesley, I looked at the book. I went back and forth. I said Wesley. When I had Wesley, it was too much for me. The doctor told him you like Katy? You want for her to live with you for a long time? Take care of her. Don't get her pregnant all the time.

Daddy wanted, to work at the shipyard at Hunter's Point in San Francisco. He would rather work there than the climate at Honolulu. That's why we came to California. Rodney bought our property (and we moved to San Francisco in August, 1958).

I didn't expect to have more children. It was in Los Angeles. I was pregnant on Renee. So, that was number five. I liked to go to Reno. When it came to Renee, I was going to name her Reno. No sooner she was born April, I got pregnant on Linda. So, Linda was born the following year, April, May, June. Like you and Kathy were so close. I loved the name Sandy. My flower girl was Sandra. Daddy liked Linda. Then I said how about Joyce? I told him that I want to name her Joyce; So, Linda Joyce.

I find my happiness that he loved to travel. He's been to Italy. He's been to Japan, China.

My mother and Cyrilla (niece) came to California after we left the islands, 1959. Mom took care of Wes and Debbie. (Cousin) Ethel came up about two weeks to one month later and stayed with my mom. We took Cyrilla, you, and Kathy to Disneyland.

I had gone to Aunty Jessie's specialist doctor. She got connection from the doctor. So, what's good for the sister is good for me too. That's how I got Dr. Tong. He told Clifford be careful. I know you enjoy sex but you got to take care of Katy. Dad had his operation, but nobody knows about it. We kept it a secret, but since you're the oldest, what's the difference? It's already done. He said that's it. I'm going to give you a break.

Linda was one year old when mom fell on the street and had a stroke. She wanted me to come back home. Dad took care of the kids while he sent me home for two weeks. My mom wanted me to stay and help her with her stroke, but I told her I couldn't. I have a family. I'm married now. My baby is just one year old.

I worked at the cannery where the tomatoes are packed making catsup. I worked at the candy factory, Jack LaLanne. All the peanut bars come out, and I can take it home and give away when I go on trips. We take trips. We go to see Debbie. We went to Canada. I went to the Chinatown over there.

One time his folks came over, and he had to go to Boston. I met him. They took care of the kids. We went to the farm to see aunty Bessie when she was living then. I got to see her again. I made a trip to see Betty Irene. I went to New York. So, I got to be out traveling again. So, I just hope that I'll be ok.

It was good to live next door to my in-laws. I got a ride to work when my mother-in-law learned how to drive. I didn't learn too much from Cliff. I got nervous and to this day, I have my children to take me around.

It's up to you guys. I try to do my best to see you guys. I'm queen, even though you have a wife. I want them to respect me too. I don't bother you guys. Well why should I? Renee don't mind doing it for me. Even Linda, once a week, bathe me. I want you and Wesley to tell his wife too to come and share and come and bathe me. I enjoy my children give me a shower.

Cliff goes on trips. He worries me. I was home with you, and you children don't sleep at somebody's house. I got train you guys to sleep on your own bed. I feel sorry that the doctor told him you don't get Katy upset because she is already downhill. You take care of her. You love her.

My life goes on. I just wait until, pau, go on trips and come back. I get the check, and I put the food money and utility money that I spend on and allowance for you kids as much as I can share with you children until later on you were old enough with part time work to help me out.

One more trip he (Cliff) was going to send me to have a good time for one month to Hong Kong but he didn't make it. He died. So, we were telling Wesley that he got to find somebody to take care of Mayah. So, he took care of Mayah and now Mayah graduate now this month. So, I am going to her graduation, and her other grandmother is going to come down too. I hope to see your son, Kayin and Tony next and sister and David and Leanna and little Jimmy.

I am planning to go back home to Hawaii, Oahu, the island I was born. I'm going to eat poke with raw fish and all kinds with the lau lau with taro leaf and octopus. I want to go. I love the food. It wouldn't be my last trip because I am waiting for my youngest grandson, Jimmy, to graduate (2007).

I have two great-grandchildren and coming this year will be the third great-grandchild. I hope Rose give a good birth. She is a wife of my grandson, Joey.

My mother is a twin. I didn't get a twin. So, my daughter, Debbie was pregnant. She had twin boys. She's married, and now she's gone. We lost her. She died of a broken heart. I kind of feel sorry for what happened. She could have lived with me. But I love my children, and she's so young that she had gone at the age of 50. Just before they closed the casket, I cried and I said, Debbie, bye. See you some day in heaven. We will put you in a nice place. Be happy, and now that you met dad, you get to play cards again.

I like to go gambling. I play blackjack. I'm good at it. My brother Raymond and Bolo is the one that helps me out. Well, mostly Chick helps me learn how to play blackjack.

I'm planning to go to Las Vegas next year for the Class of '46 reunion (60th). I am going to contact the president for information and go to Honolulu in March. I go spend three weeks there.

I have all my good teeth. I lost some teeth from caps with Dr. Yuen all these years. Daddy wanted partials too. He didn't want his whole teeth taken out. Recently, I got lower partials from Dr. Chin. I'm not used to the way he make it. You got to take it out at night and put it back in the morning. I don't have the coordination.

My sister-in law; she's still living. I'm going to fight for it if I can but no use. I know that Mayrose did take care of my mother and father. I'm still angry with her for taking the house away from us. To this day, she doesn't know who to give the house to. Her twins don't want the house. Now her grandchildren kind of take over the house but she made a will. She's not going to kick them out of the house. They're going to remodel it. Termites already got into the house, but I don't care. I'm still angry with her for what she's done.

When I suffered a stroke, Clifford (grandson) knew that something was wrong. He first discovered that my face was kind of droopy. I try to balance my foot.

I don't know how long I'm going to live. I thought dad would be alive, a second vow for our marriage. That was my way, but he died. I just hope that daddy is waiting for me. Now that he passed away, he's joined by my Debbie and she now joined the dad. They can play Japanese cards. I don't know how to play that game. I let him play with Debbie when he was alive. Now that he's gone, he has my Debbie now. That keeps him busy

Epilogue

February 18, 2009, was the last recording that I made when she was at Park Central Care and Rehabilitation Center in Fremont, California. She was admitted there on September 13, 2006, a year after I first recorded her at her residence at 28111 East 12th Street, Hayward, California.

She was having ongoing trouble swallowing and couldn't get enough food or liquids by mouth. She had a procedure called percutaneous endoscopic gastrostomy (PEG). The tube allows feeding directly into the gastrointestinal tract to occur by bypassing the mouth and esophagus.

"I was losing weight on a diet. I went to the hospital Tuesday. The doctor put me out and then I didn't feel anything. They cut. It took me five hours. The doctor gave me couple stitches. He fixed me up."

In remembrance from Linda: "What I remembered about mom was when she had people come visit and eat with her and when she did eat with us. Also, to see that smile on her face when we visited her and go take her for a walk. That smile was priceless when we will visit her every week."

Addendum

Excerpt from my brother Wes's timeline notes:

07/22/2005- Mom emergency overnight stay, CT scan, unknown, possible stroke

07/11/2006- Evening: mom emergency, high temperature, urinary infection, antibiotics

07/23/2006- 07:30 AM: ambulance, admitted, high temperature, urinary infection, stronger antibiotics

07/25/2006- Home: 01:30 AM; fall, 03:30 PM; fall

08/06/2006- Home: 01:00 AM; fall, 04:00 AM; fall

09/12/2006- Went on a bus tour to Thunder Valley Casino Resort in Lincoln with her friend, Val. While walking to the bus, she pressed the hand brakes on her walker to stop and lost her balance. She hit her head on the concrete pavement. An ambulance rushed her to Kaiser Hospital Emergency in Roseville and she stayed overnight. They were going to send her to a rehabilitation facility in Roseville. The tour bus unknowingly had left without her. Wes drove up to Roseville to pick her up. Both Wes and Renee made arrangements to admit her locally. She was taken to Park Central Care and Rehabilitation in Fremont. Due to her unsteadiness, and not being able to take care of herself, it was determined that she be admitted. We had a family discussion, and mom willingly agreed to stay 24/7 care.

Chung Poon Leong, grandpa

Moi See, grandma

Name: Jeong Yuk Lin
Age: 8   Height: 4' 2-1/2"
Occupation: Student
Local residence: Kukui St., Honolulu, Oahu, T.H.
Physical marks and peculiarities: None visible
   Issued in the Territory of Hawaii, this 5
day of August 1906

mom, Norman, dad
Circa 1916

Raymond, Richard (Bolo), Koon Suan, Mom, Katherine

(7) (5) (3) (29) (1)
1929

CERTIFICATE OF LIVE BIRTH

STATE OF HAWAII
DEPARTMENT OF HEALTH

CERTIFICATE NO. **151 1928 - 008501**

DECEASED

CHILD'S NAME
KATHERINE   KOON HUNG   CHUN

DATE OF BIRTH
February 27, 1928

HOUR OF BIRTH
7:00 PM

SEX
FEMALE

CITY, TOWN OR LOCATION OF BIRTH
HONOLULU

ISLAND OF BIRTH
OAHU

COUNTY OF BIRTH
HONOLULU

MOTHER'S MAIDEN NAME
CHEONG   YUCK   LIN

MOTHER'S RACE
CHINESE

FATHER'S NAME
CHOCK   CHUN

FATHER'S RACE
CHINESE

DATE FILED BY REGISTRAR
March 10, 1928

OHSM 1.2 (Rev 10/14) LASER   This copy serves as prima facie evidence of the fact of birth in any court proceeding. [HRS 338-13(b), 338-19]

ANY ALTERATIONS INVALIDATE THIS CERTIFICATE

STANDARD CERTIFICATE OF BIRTH
TERRITORY OF HAWAII

File No. 9090

1. **PLACE OF BIRTH** — County: Honolulu, State: T.H., City: Honolulu
2. **Full name of child:** Mary Foon Yong Chun
3. **Sex:** Female
6. **Premature:** Full term
7. **Legitimate:** Yes
8. **Date of birth:** March 9, 1930

FATHER
9. **Full name:** Chock Chun
10. **Residence:** Honolulu, T.H.
11. **Color or Race:** Chinese
12. **Age at last birthday:** 43 years
13. **Birthplace:** China
14. **Trade, profession:** Manager
15. **Industry or business:** Wing Ho Laundry
17. **Total time (years) spent in this work:** 17 yrs

MOTHER
18. **Full maiden name:** Yuck Lin Cheong
19. **Residence:** Honolulu
20. **Color or Race:** Chinese
21. **Age at last birthday:** 32 years
22. **Birthplace:** Honolulu, Oahu, T.H.
23. **Trade, profession:** Housekeeper
24. **Industry or business:** own home

27. **Number of children of this mother:** (a) Born alive and now living: 6 (b) Born alive but now dead: 2 (c) Stillborn: 0

29a. **Was a prophylactic for ophthalmia neonatorum used?** Yes — Silver nitrate

CERTIFICATE OF ATTENDING PHYSICIAN
I hereby certify that I attended the birth of this child, who was born alive at 1 A.m. on the date above stated.

(Signed) T. H. Kong, M.D., Physician
Address: 525 S. _____ St.

Date Recorded (or Registered): APR - 9 1930
Date Filed, Office of Registrar General: APR - 9 1930

APR 24 1930

My wedding Sunday March 21, 1948
Original group wedding picture was taken in black and white, then filled in with colored pencils.

4048 KAIMUKI AVENUE	Carol & Rodney Wong
4048-A	Mary & Leonard H. Wong
4048-B	Katherine & Clifford K. C. Wong

Our first home, purchased in 1948 for $10,000 each.
We sold it to Rodney for $12,000 in 1958.
In April 1991, the property was valued at $740,000

Cliff planted the first seed in 1951

The First Fruit

1952

Mary, mom, aunty Ah Yuk, Katy

Waiting to depart United DC-7 plane from
Honolulu Airport to San Francisco, California
August 1958

Katy, Wes, Cliff
Debbie, Dennis, Kathy

Oct. 15, 1958
Kathleen is wearing All Hallow School uniform
Kathleen and Dennis were ready to go to school
so I took this picture before they went to school.

Mar. 1959
The horse and the bull are bought in Tijuana, Mexico.
The lilies plant was given to us by our friend in
Oakland for Easter. We invited him to dinner
on Easter Eve.

Mom came to visit us

64 Hilltop Rd. San Francisco

December 1959

27098 St. Francis Avenue, Hayward, California- May 8, 1965. Built in 1958 and sold for $15,999. We purchased it in 1960 for $17,999 from Joe Texeira. Sold in 1991 for $160,000.

Celebrating Renee's 14th
April 8, 1974

Christmas 1975

13 Dec 75

Dear Dennis & Kimmy,

Received two xmas cards from the family. One from you and one from mommy. Thank you all very much. We are not sending out cards this year. Xmas is not like it used to be. We are not having a good xmas this year for my sister Mom is in the hospital and might have to have her foot amputated. Only the good Lord can save her foot. She is leaving it all in his care.

Friday while coming home from visiting her at the hospital we got into an accident. My niece Fran was driving and I was on the passenger's side. A car making a left turn hit our car on the left side. We were not badly hurt only lumps (two) on the head and bruise on the back (left shoulder). We didn't have to go to the hospital, thank god.

Now for the question. I mailed the certificates so you can see the dates. Kalaki Kung Kwong and Apo was married sometime in 1914 or very early in 1915. That was Chinese (Buddhist) marriage which was legal here and married American style in may 1924. Really don't know much about it. Also the names are very confusing. Apo's name is Yuk Lin Jong, but under Chuck's birth certificate, has her as Yuk Lin Chang.

Anyway we wish you all a very merry Xmas and a happy new year. Our love to the girls and mommy and daddy.

If you folks have Wesley's address please send it to us. Would like to write to him.

Love,
Aunty Marjorie & family

P.S. This is for mommy
Dear Katherine,
Received your card and thanks alot. Will not be sending out cards this year. Just can't get started and don't have the spirit. It seems like every year it gets harder to shop for the holidays. Uncle Chickie sends his love to Renée. All our love to you and family.
Aloha,
Marjorie

JET-ON TRAVEL SERVICE, INC.

MANDARIN TOWER ARCADE
899 WASHINGTON STREET
SAN FRANCISCO, CALIFORNIA 94108
PHONES (415) 433-4415   433-4416
CABLE ADDRESS: JETON SAN FRANCISCO, CALIFORNIA

RE: SEPT. 25, 1982 - JET-ON CHINA (BEIJING) TOUR

Dear Tour Members,

WELCOME to our CHINA (BEIJING) group tour. While you are on your way to BEIJING on board PAN AM's 747, please read the following information:

1. This PAN-AM flight (PA011) will bring you to Narita, Japan, arriving on Sept. 25, 1982 at 4:40pm. At Narita Airport, we will connect to Pan Am flight #015 at 6:00pm. Your arrival date in BEIJING will be Sept. 26, 1982 at 9:35pm.

2. To enable us to operate your tour as smoothly as possible, we would appreciate your on-time performance and at the direction of your Tour Leader. We are pleased to advise that Mr. Paul Ko will be your Tour Leader.

3. Inside your ticket jacket, a health form, a Chinese Custom form, an Entry & Exit form for China and a Hong Kong entry form are provided for your convenience. Please complete them where necessary and sign your name at the appropriate place.

4. Your returning flight, if booked, will be re-confirmed by your Tour Leader as indicated in your airticket. If not, you could make your own reservations with Pan Am directly in Hong Kong. The phone # is (5) 231111.

5. Please safe-keep your Passport and Air Ticket at ALL TIMES. SHOPPING is done entirely at your own risk; use your good judgement in your purchases. Eat light, drink more fluids, and sleep early is the best way to keep you healthy throughout.

6. Your stay at the Excelsior Hotel in Hong Kong has been made per your instructions. Please pay direct to Excelsior when checking-out.

7. On your return (Hong Kong/San Francisco), airport tax is HK$20.00 per person is required. Please pay direct to Pan American at the airport.

8. DUTY FREE purchases for returning U.S. Residents is US$300.00 per person. Any excess will be subject to the rules and regulations of the U.S. Customs.

Thank you all once again for your kind assistance and cooperation in this matter. Meanwhile, we wish all of you a very PLEASANT trip. BON VOYAGE!

With Best Regards.

Yours sincerely,
JET-ON TRAVEL SERVICE, INC.

S.Y. Mak, President

YOUR SATISFACTION IS OUR GOAL

MON Sept 27 Tour zoo - Summer Palace. Symphony night
Tues " 28 Ming Tombs - Great Wall. Acrobat stage show
Wed " 29 Yung He Gong Lama Temple - Red Sports ass exhibition
Thur " 30 Tien an Men (Gate of Heavenly Peace) - Mao Tse Tung
       Forbidden City. Night Peking Duck Dinner (Peking)
Fri Nanking Forbidden City, Sun Yat Sen Mausoleum
Sat Moo Hou Lake Yank-Tse River Bridge Old City Gate
(Sun Wuxin) Visit China Pottery Lake on Ferry, Fishing
Monkey) Factory
Mon Soochow doll factory Embroidery factory Park
Tues — Park sandlewood factory (Park) Lake Villa & Humble
                                                Garden
       Mistress PR West Garden. Water Topped Pagoda - shopping
Wed walk around the lake
Thur Shanghai boat excursion, schools
Fri Arrive late in Hangchow silk factory
Sat Visit temple, garden and lake
Sun went western temple. Shops boat 1 hour. boat excursion
      and walk around the lake. (west lake)
Mon Kwei Lin arrive after lunch. Visit the seven
     star cave did a lot of walking
Tues Visit Yueyai Shuan (Piled Silk hill) Flower cave
     Elephant Trunk Hill, and Art Crafts Factory.
     Night Chinese Acrobatic Talent Show.
Wed. Ferry boat ride on River Lishang River. Shop
     for about an hour at end of ride
Thu Silk Factory

Zarek's graduation June 2004

Tennyson High School Hayward, CA

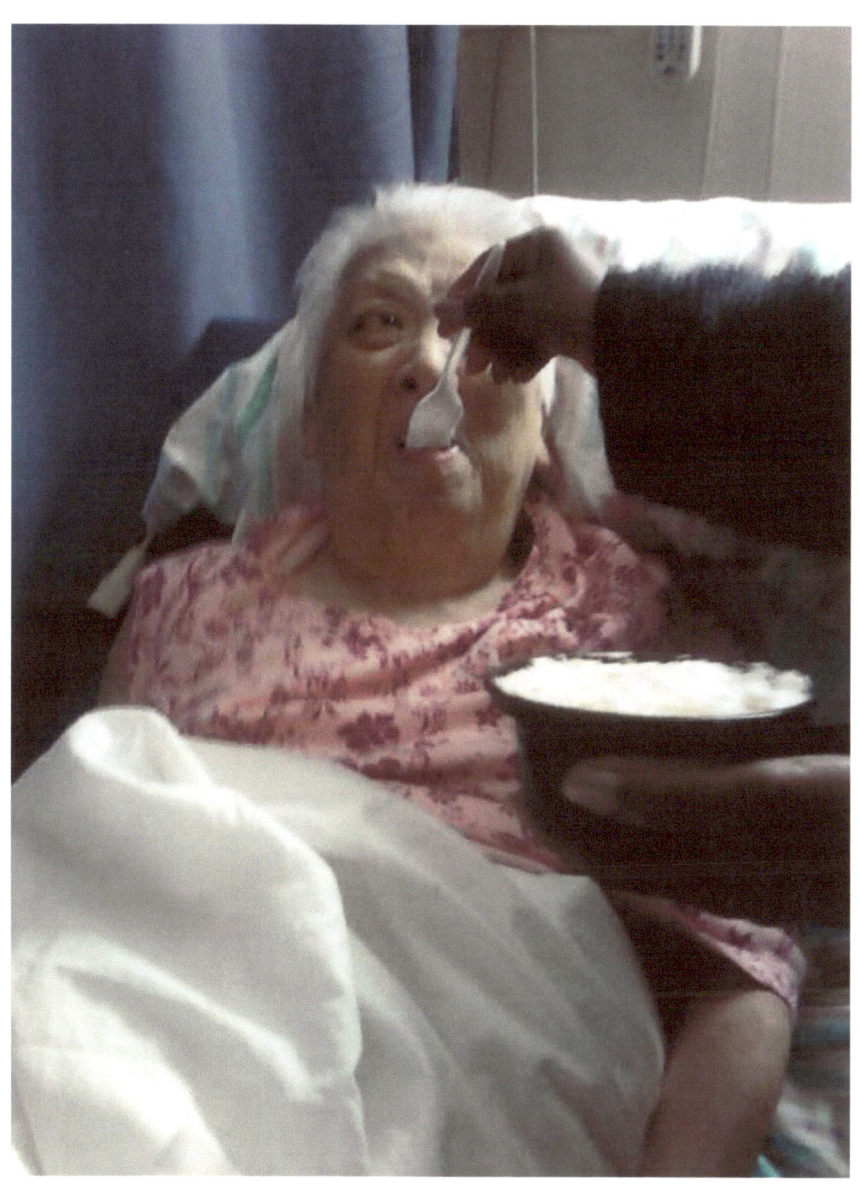

83rd-Jocelyn feeding me my birthday cake
Sunday February 27, 2011

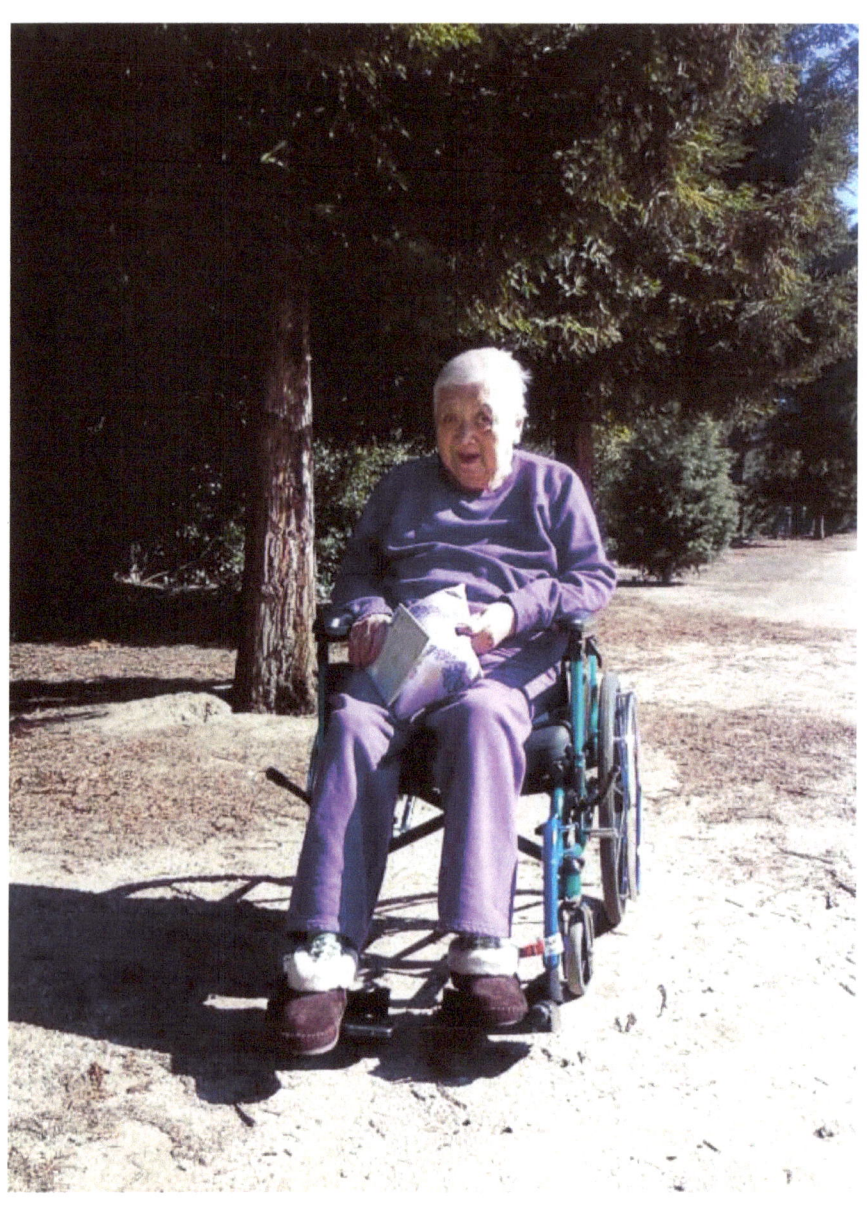

Outing with Dennis at Parkmont Elementary School
May 8, 2011

CLIFFORD KWEI CHONG WONG - KATHERINE KOON HUNG CHUN
王桂祥　　　　　　　　　陳觀杏
10/6/1923　　　　　　　　2/27/1928

DENNIS	KATHLEEN	DEBORAH	WESLEY	RENEE	LINDA JOYCE
WAI CHUNG	MEW LUNG	SAU LUNG	WAI HONG	NGIT LUNG	YUKE LUNG
王惠鐘	王妙玲	王秀玲	王惠康	王月玲	王玉玲
11/6/1951	1/8/1953	10/18/1954	3/23/1956	4/8/1960	6/29/1961

My Wedding

Katherine Chun, Clifford Wong Wed in Sunday Service

Calla lilies were the predominant flowers in the First Chinese Church of Christ for the marriage of Miss Katherine K. H. Chun and Clifford K. C. Wong.

The Couple exchanged vows March 21 with the Rev. Charles Kwock officiating.

Daughter of Mr. and Mrs. Chock Chun, 2309 Kanealii Ave., the bride was given in marriage by her father. She wore a heavy white satin gown and jade necklace.

Her veil was caught to a crown of apple blossoms. She carried large white cattleya orchids.

Miss Mary K. Y. Chun, the bride's sister, was maid of honor. She was gowned in yellow brocaded taffeta with a complimenting bird of paradise bouquet.

Bridesmaids were Miss Jennie Look and Miss Wilma Jeong. They wore green and blue brocaded taffeta gowns respectively. Like the maid of honor, they wore sweetheart hats.

Flower girl was Miss Sandra Lee. She wore a pink taffeta gown.

The bridegroom, son of Mr. and Mrs. Leonard H. Wong, 3247 Hayden St., chose his brother, Walter K. S. Wong, as best man.

Ushers were Tom Mizunaka and Raymond Chang.

The bride's mother wore a lavender print Chinese gown with a white cattleya orchid corsage. The bridegroom's mother wore a gray print Chinese gown, also complimented by a white orchid corsage.

A reception followed at the home of the bridegroom's parents.

After a 10 day honeymoon in Hilo, the bridal pair are now living in Honolulu.

The bride, a McKinley high school graduate, is employed at the controller's office.

The bridegroom is employed at the navy yard. He was graduated from Farrington high school.

In Memory of

Katherine
Obituary

Clifford
"My Dad"

Debbie
"Adorned Beauty"

KATHERINE C. WONG
February 27, 1928 - July 20, 2014

Katherine (Katy) C. Wong
Resident of Hayward

 Katy passed away on Sunday of natural causes at the age of 86. Katy was born in Honolulu, HI, graduated from McKinkley High School in 1946. She was a homemaker most of her life. When Katy was nine or ten, she worked at the family's laundry business in Kakaako. After Katy got married, she worked at the controller's office at Alexander Young Hotel. She moved to Hayward in 1960, worked at the Hunt-Wesson cannery, and later at a candy factory where they made Jack LaLanne Hi-Protein bars and at American Drapery.
 Katy is survived by her devoted children Dennis Wong (Jocelyn) of Hayward, Kathleen (Kathy) Vernon (Larry) of Grover Beach, Wesley Wong (Simona) of Union City, Renee Nasario (Gerald) of Hayward, Linda Joyce Carvallyo (James) of Hayward and 14 grandchildren and 10 great-grandchildren, preceded in death by her husband Clifford Wong and her daughter Deborah (Debbie) Weise. She is also survived by her sister Mary Jay of Honolulu, HI. Her generous loving spirit will be missed by all who knew her. Friends and family are invited to a visitation and funeral service on Sunday July 27, 2014 at 09:00 a.m. to 02:00 p.m. Burial to follow.
(510) 471-3363

Cemetery
Chapel of the Chimes Memorial Park
32992 Mission Boulevard
Hayward, CA, 94544

My Dad
By
Paul Peterson

He isn't much in the eyes of the world; He'll never make history.
No, he isn't much in the eyes of the world, But he is the world to me.

My dad, now here is a man.
To me he is ev'rything strong; no he can't do wrong, my dad.
My dad, now he understands when I bring him troubles to share;
Oh, he's always there, my dad.
When I was small I felt ten feet tall.
When I walked by his side
And ev'ry one would say, "that's his son,"
and my heart would burst with pride.
My dad, oh, I love him so,
And I only hope that some day my own son will say,
"My dad, now here is a man."

In Loving Memory
To My Sister Debbie
October 18, 1954 - May 06, 2005

"Adorned Beauty"

Adorned beauty,
Natural as can be,
Precious for all to see,
In spirit, you are free.

Remembering yesterday,
Reminiscing this May.
Remembering the years,
The unknown and the fears.
Remembering all that you meant,
And the brief times that we spent.
Remembering our birthday exchanges,
Over the distant mountain ranges.
Remembering your new outlook,
And the path that you took.

A new beginning unravels;
Go placidly in your travels.
Losing you is sad,
But now you're with dad.

Big Brother,
Dennis

Ephesians 1:18

I pray also that the eyes of your heart may be enlightened
in order that you may know
the hope to which he has called you,
the riches of his glorious inheritance of the saints.

BEYOND
THE APRICOT OUTLOOK

Recent visit to Honolulu

I traveled to Honolulu, Hawaii from October 8th through the 11th 2018. Prior to my trip, I subscribed to Newspaper.com and printed some newspaper articles from The Honolulu Advertiser on Chung Chock, my mother's father. I shared copies with my cousins Norma and Brandon Wong, Donna Tateishi, Darlene Heu, Hermanelle Shinkawa, and Aunty Mary.

The following were clipped from The Honolulu Advertiser:

29 March 1922 Wednesday page 7 **Wing Hoon**, five-year old son of Mr. and Mrs. Chung Chock of Second and Keawe Streets, Kakaako, died in Kauikeolani Children's hospital last Monday from diphteria. The young boy was a native of this city and was buried yesterday in Pauoa Chinese cemetary.

20 May 1924, Tuesday page 5: **Chung-Chong**—In Honolulu, May 17, 1924 Chung Chock and Miss Chang Yick Lin, Rev. Robert Ahuna officiating; witnesses—En Yate Pung and Chuu Kong.

11 February 1926, Thursday page 5: **Chun**—In Honolulu, January 21, 1926, to Mr. and Mrs. Chock Chun, Second, near Keawe Street, Kakaako, on March 9, Kakaako, a daughter—Koon Suan.

10 April 1930, Thursday page 9 Mary Koon Yong is the name given by Mr. and Mrs. Chock Chun to a daughter born at their home, Second, near Keawe street, Kakaako, on March 9. Chun is manager of the Wing Wo Laundry.

12 January 1933, Thursday page 2 Chinese Chamber to Raise Funds Money to Aid Sufferers in Manchuria Is Sought
Fourteen platoons of solicitors took the field yesterday, according to announcement from the United Chinese society and the Chinese chamber of commerce, to raise funds for the relief of suffering in Manchuria and the northeastern provinces of China generally.
The solicitors for the first group are Wong Tuck Yee and Liang Hung Sung; the second group, Chun Kow, Samuel K. Young, Wong Buck Hung and Yuen Poy; the third, Lee Akau, Hoo Tai and Chun How; the fourth, Tom Quay, Chow Tim Kau and Lee Sau Chong; the fifth, Chang Fung Kee and Leong Boo; the sixth, Leong Chew, Chun Kim Chow and Henry Siu; the seventh, Wong Lum, Lee Tim and Tom Tai Leong.
The eighth, Chee Yick Young, Leong Han and Hee Cho; the ninth, Siu Chu Hee and Fong Kim Yet; the 10th, C. Chocks Hing, Chang Ho Leong and Chang Hing; the 11th, Lum Ki Chung, Chun Kung Lum, Given Tang and Lau See Hing; the 12th, Lau Tong and Lee Lai Chin; the 13th, Lee Len, Chow Wah Say, Lum Yung Kin and Lee Kee; the 14th, Lum Chong, Yee See Kau and Chun Tin Bow.
All the donations will be collected once a month and forwarded to the national council for relief work in the northeastern provinces, with the headquarters in Shanghai. The local organization is a branch of this national council.

2 June 1942, Tuesday page 9   Laundry Here Razed By Fire—The Wing Wo Laundry, 650 Keawe street, in Kakaako, was destroyed by fire Sunday night. The fire is believed to have started in the wash house only six feet away from the main building. The laundry was not covered by insurance. Chung Chock, 2309 Kanealii street, owned the establishment.

15 September 1949, Thursday page 8   NOTICE OF DISSOLUTION OF CO-PARTNERSHIP—Notice is hereby given that on the 31st day of August, 1949, the undersigned agreed to dissolve the co-partnership known under the name and style of Iwilei Chop Suey maintaining and carrying on a Restaurant Business at 804 Iwilei Road, Honolulu, Hawaii. Witness our hands this 30th day of August, 1949.

        (S) **CHUNG CHOCK**
        (S) **MICHAEL P. L. CHUN**
        (S) **KAM HEONG CHUN**

3 January 1950, Tuesday page 8   Federick Chun is elected Head of Chun clan. Frederick K.T. Chun, manager of the Kim Chow Shoe Store, Nuuanu Ave., was recently elected president of the local Chun Clan society for 1949.
He was inaugurated Monday at a New Year luncheon at the society's clubhouse on N. School St.
Other New Officers of the society, which is known as Chun Wing Chin Tong to local Chinese, are:
Vice president, Tin Bow Chun; treasurer, Sau Yick Chun; assistant treasurer Harry K. Chun; recording secretary, Yit Ming Chun; vice, Tit Heong Chun, Chinese secretary, Dai Kee Chun; auditor, Dai Chun; assistant, Sik Kong Chun.

14 February 1952, Thursday page 7
Chun clan will meet for dinner Saturday night.
About 300 Honolulans with the surname Chun will meet at Wo Fat Sunday at 4:30 p.m. at a dinner sponsored by the Chun Wing Chin Tong of which Yee Sing Chun is president. The organization comprises 3,000 Hawaii residents with the surname Chun.
The Society president and Council General T.S.Y. Tonglao will speak and Chun Kung Lum will be master of ceremonies. A musical program has been arranged by Chun Leong Gee and will feature Mandarin and Cantonese selections by the Ching Wun Dramatic and Musical club headed by Ng Kam Yuen and Tai Leong Yim.
Solo numbers will be given by Siu Tan Ching and Yick Cho Chui. The Narcissus queen, Wanda Chang, will be present.
The Organization is a benevolent society with headquarters on Stillman lan. Henry Chun-Hoon is honorary president.
Other officers are:
Ken How Chun, vice president; Frederick K.C. Chun, treasurer; Harry K. Chun, assistant treasurer; Leong Chee Chun, Chinese corresponding secretary; Koong Lum Chin, assistant Chinese corresponding secretary; Sam Loy Chun, English secretary; Yet Ming Chun, Chinese recording secretary; Wai Cheong Chun, assistant Chinese recording secretary; Tin Bow Chun, auditor; Jou Sin Chun, assistant auditor; Dai Chun, bookkeeper; Sau Yick Chun, assistant bookkeeper; Kwock Moy Chun and Buck Ing Chun, sergeant-at-arms, and Attorney Leon Chun, legal adviser.

3 August 1952, Sunday page 27   Honolulu's 'Little Merchants' –Mrs. Kam Heong Chun is Partner in Hand Laundry By Curtis Otani:

Among the first group of "little merchants" to establish businesses in Honolulu were the Chinese. The Chinese community, now preparing for the centennial celebration of the arrival here of the first group of Chinese laborers, points with pride to the part their group has played in the progress of the territory.

Many Chinese merchants, including the "little ones," have contributed greatly to local economic development. The latter includes the small neighborhood grocery and general merchandise stores and other businesses in many sections of Honolulu. Today, however, only a few such stores are operated by Chinese

UNLIKE MOST OF their parents, Americans of Chinese ancestry have gone into diversified fields of business and, as a result, when the founders of the small stores retired, no one in the family continued the "family store."

The younger people are no longer attracted to the type of business their parents operated for many years, with long working hours and small profits.
Mrs. Kam Heong Chun, a partner of Wo Lung Laundry at 1216 Emma St., says "Nowadays, the young people don't want to go into this kind of business, because they don't want to work long hours. I remember in the old days when we used to work 12 to 14 hours a day, including Sundays

Even now Mrs. Chun opens her shop at 7 a.m. and closes at 5 p.m. She has been in the laundry business for 30 years.

"WHEN WE WERE YOUNG, there was no compulsory educational system in Hawaii, so I had hardly any education," she recalls.

She worked in her father's tailor shop until she was married, and after her marriage she went to work in a laundry which was operated by her brother-in-law.

The Wing Wo laundry, which was owned by Chock Chun, opened for business in 1915 on Keawe St. in Kakaako. Business was good and it later became one of the largest in the city. But in 1942 the plant was burned down, and she was out of a job.

She took a rest for a while, then worked as a cook in a cafeteria at Pearl Harbor for a year. After that she did various odd jobs in the city for several years.

IN 1947 SHE OPENED a chop suey restaurant in Iwilei in partnership with her brother-in law and operated it successfully for two years. However, they agreed they needed a rest, so they sold the restaurant and decided to retire. But no sooner had they retired than they became restless doing nothing and again formed a partnership and took over the laundry business at the present location.

"You'd never believe it, but between us we had only $400 to start the business," she says. As her brother-in-law is now too old to work full time at the laundry, Mrs. Chun operates the business with the help of her nephew.

The Missing Link in China

My journey continued into China the following week on October 20th through the 26th 2018. I attended a Chinese Genealogy class in Las Vegas on January 29 through the 31st 2018 which was presented by Henry Tom. During one of the afternoon rounds session, I met a woman, Mel Young. I showed her an affidavit from the **Department of Commerce and Labor Immigration Service** of my grandfather Chong Chock. He tried to claim that he was of Hawaiian birth.

Mel looked at his signature and said that it was also a Chan surname. Then she told me about looking up my village at http://villagedb.friendsofroots.org/search.cgi. She searched for Chan villages and found Sam Hop Heung which contains 89 villages. I scrolled down the list and saw a village named Sheung Ning. The affidavit had listed his village as Sew Ning, Sam Kop, Canton, China.

Henry asked a friend, Douglas Lam, who is from Zhongshan and knows the LongDu dialect to find my ancestral villages. He now lives in Sydney, Australia and takes a month vacation each year to help Chinese-Americans find their roots.

I also met Gail Chong at the seminar. I told her about Douglas. She was interested in joining Douglas and me to assist in her search for her villages and also help translate. Gail's cousin, Gee Sing, was used as our driver for our trip and he was paid for his service.

On October 25, we drove to Taishan County, formerly romanized in Cantonese as Toishan, in local dialect as Hoisan or Toisan, and formerly known as Xinning or Sunning. It is a county-level city in the southwest of Guangdong province and it is administered as part of the prefecture-level city of Jiangmen. Taishan calls itself the "First home of the overseas Chinese. From our Zhongshan International Hotel, it was an hour and a half ride to Taishan.

Then we headed to Sam Hop area. We located Sheung Ning. It was a small village with about 8 houses. We asked the local villagers if they knew a person by the name of Chung Chock. No one there could help us and said maybe we can check the next village. There was a Chung Chock listed in the next village. He previously resided there but moved about 12 to 14 years ago and is still alive. This Chung Chock had a second name.

I called my cousin, Norma in Hawaii to ask her if she knows our grandfather's second name. Because of the time difference, I was hesitant on calling her. It was 11:59 p.m. Hawaii time. Without Chung Chock's second name, we had not much to go on. So, I called and apologized on waking her up. I was hoping she may be able to shed some light that could help before we left the village.

On all the old newspaper articles that I read, only Chung Chock, Chun Chock, or Chun Tin Bow were printed. Chinese men can have up to 7 different names (birth, marriage, profession, etc.). Dr. Sun Yat Sen had 7 names. Chung Chock was a member of the Chun clan and a former vice-president and auditor of the See Yup Benevolent Society. This society served members descending from three villages in China. He is buried in the Manoa Chinese Cemetery under the name Chun Tin Bow. We drove back that evening and I flew back home the next morning. If I find additional information, I may be back next year. As the local villagers are getting older, it makes it difficult to find any of the present younger generation who can help us.

AFFIDAVIT in support of claim of Chung Chock to Hawaiian birth of said Chung Chock. Chung Choon being first duly sworn, on oath deposes and says that he is 45 years of age, and has resided in the Hawaiian Islands for 25 years, that he is the brother (by the same father and mother) of Chung Poon Leong formally of Honolulu Island of Oahu Territory of Hawaii, that affiant knows well Chung Chock, his nephew, applicant aforesaid; that affiant saw said Chung Chock on the day of the latter's birth, to wit about December 25, 1887, at the place of the latter's birth on King Street, near what is now Aala Park, in said Honolulu and saw said Chung Chock as often as once a week until said Chung Chock was about three years old, when the said Chung Poon Leong took said Chung Chock to China; that in 1894 and during about one year thereafter affiant saw said Chung Chock at Sew Ning, Sam Kop, Canton, China, with the father Chung Poon Leong and the mother Moi See; that in 1899 affiant being then in Honolulu received from said Chung Poon Leong notice of the intended departure of said Chung Chock to Honolulu aforesaid by a certain steamer whose names affiant does not now remember, and thereafter affiant met the said Chung Chock at Honolulu Harbor aforesaid on the arrival of said steamer there and on the release of said Chung Chock from quarantine; that affiant then recognized the said Chung Chock as the same person born in Honolulu about December 25, 1887, and of whom the photograph hereto annexed is a good likeness at the present time.

**Sworn to and subscribed before me this
_____ Day** of December, **1908**

Attached to this affidavit was an application for card of identification:

Hawaii, December 21ˢᵗ, 1908

To the Inspector in Charge,
    United States Immigration Service,
        Territory of Hawaii.

    Sir: I hereby make application for **CARD OF IDENTIFICATION**, authorized to be issued under Regulations of the Department of Commerce and Labor, approved January 14, 1908, to Chinese persons or persons of Chinese descent born in the Hawaiian Islands, and to Chinese persons or persons of Chinese descent who were naturalized as citizens of Hawaii prior to annexation of said islands to the United States, and I hereby certify that I am entitled to such card of identification by reason of being a person of Chinese descent born in the Hawaiian Islands in substantiation of which I submit herewith the following documentary proofs and affidavit, or **affidavits**: affidavit of Chung Choon, and certified copy of certificate of Hawaiian birth (application no 237) issued to me July 27, 1908 by the Secretary of the Territory of Hawaii.

Name by which commonly known: Chung Chock
All other names by which known: no other names or name

                              Age: 20 years last birthday
                                          nearly 21 years

Occupation: night watchman Quarantine Island Honolulu Harbor United States Marine Hospital Service, Island of Oahu Territory of Hawaii

Where born: King Street Honolulu   **Date of birth:** December 25, 1887

Present local residence: at Quarantine Island aforesaid

Height: about 5 feet, 9 ½ inches, without shoes

Physical marks and peculiarities: small scar above left side of right eyebrow.

Signature in Chinese:

Signature in English:

"My China Roots" Research

From: Miao Hai <haimiao@mychinaroots.com>
Sent: Wed, Aug 10, 2016 3:33 am
Subject: 答复: 答复: Chung Chock's Research

Hi Dennis,
The challenge is, we only know his Chinese name, but no his parents' name. Chung Chock is a short name and no generation character in the middle. In tradition, Chinese people named their children following a poem made by the whole clan, one generation pick up one character from that poem, the next generation pick up the next character in the poem. So, normally people have the same middle character in the same clan. Due to Zhongshan has more than 20 villages that all the villagers are surnamed Chen, and Chen is a big surname in china, lots of other villages also have Chen people. So it is really hard to find where Chung Chock was from.

About the address Sew Ning, Sam Kow, we checked the local gazetteers to find places similar as this pronunciation. We found Sanjiao Town, but failed there and haven't found any new places.

Why we choose Zhongshan as our main research place, that Zhongshan has the most population which migrated to Hawaii in Guangdong.

The next step, we will continue work with Historical Society of Zhongshan, and expend searching area if we still can't find any information.

We will keep you update once we get any news!

Warm regards,

Haimiao

February 9, 2017
Hi Dennis,
For the research, we have got the feedback from the village, they didn't find any people would match Chung Chock. But, from the local government, we found out a Oo Syak Gee Lu Society in Hawaii. They may have some old records of the Zhongshan people who migrated to Hawaii. The local officer gave us two contacts from it, I attached the name cards with this email. Maybe you could contact them to see if there are any chance.

It is a great pity of the failure that we didn't managed to find the home village of Chung Chock. We would be very happy to help you if you have any other needs.

Best regards,

Haimiao

Who I Am

I am the 7th child of Chock Chung and Yuk Lin Jeong. My father was born in Sew Ning village, Sam Kop heung, Taishan, Guangdong, China on December 25, 1887 and died on March 1, 1953 in Honolulu, HI from coronary infarction and chronic nephritis. The birthdate of December 25th is from his affidavit in 1908 witnessed by uncle Choon but December 5th is the date on his obituary and gravestone. My mother was born on August 2, 1899 in Honolulu, HI and died on Wednesday March 4, 1970 at 11:50 p.m.at her home in Honolulu from massive cerebral hemorrhage, diabetes mellitus, and hypertensive cardio-vascular disease. She was the eldest of 2 sets of twin girls. Her twin sister was Gum Yuk (Ah Yuk).

My grandparents selected two suitors for my mother and her twin sister, Ah Yuk, but my mother did not like the man, who was chosen for her. Since she was the eldest twin, she got to choose and her sister married the man, who was intended for her. My mother and Ah Yuk had a Chinese Buddhist double wedding ceremony on June 23, 1915 when they were 15 years old. A Buddhist wedding is a marriage based on spiritual faith where both couples vow to maintain a harmonious and spiritual sound relationship. The entire marriage ceremony is treated more like a social affair. My parents had an American wedding on May 17, 1924.They operated a Chinese Laundry business, Wing Wo, in the Kakaako district in Honolulu, Hi in the 1930's at 650 Keawe Street. The laundry business was destroyed by fire and is believed to have started in the wash house on Sunday May 31, 1942.

On my paternal side, my grandparents were Poon Leong Chung and Moi See. He was a tailor and had a store on Nuuanu Street, just above King Street. A fire started at his store and was pretty well gutted on Monday March 3, 1891.

On my maternal side, my grandparents were On Jeong and Wong Shee. My grandfather was born in 1850 and came from Sun Wui of the See Yup district, Guangdong province, China and was one of the first Chinese laborers to come to the island of Kauai and was 18 years old at the time. His picture bride, Wong Shee, came from Canton, China several years later. She was born in 1875 and died Thursday December 20, 1923. They had 10 children, all born in Honolulu. He operated a tailor shop on Hotel Street which was wiped out by the Chinatown fire. He later established an herb in shop at 116 Hotel Street.

My uncles were Chung Chan, Wai Sun, and Bing Loy. My aunties were Kam Han, Gum Yuk (Ah Yuk), twins Mew Hou and Mew Yung, and Jun Hou (Alice). There was another aunty who was adopted and taken to China. Her name was unknown.

Chung Chan,68, of 508 Kunawai Lane was born on September 26, 1897 and died on Friday August 1, 1966 at St. Francis Hospital. He was a retired pharmacist at American Drug Company.

Wai Sun was born on December 28, 1901 and died Saturday morning March 27, 1954 at the family home, 2280 Makanani Drive. He had been under hospitalization for six months for a heart ailment. Wai Sun was a former proprietor of the Singapore Bar and past president of the Kong Chow Society. He was also a member of the See Yup Benevolent Society, Yi Yee Tong, and the American Chinese Club. He married Clarice C. On December 5, 1945, a fight erupted at the entrance to the Singapore Bar at 304 N. King St. It involved Wai Sun, manager, who was acting as doorman, and a Seaman, who was refused admittance. He punched Wai Sun and then kicked him after he had fallen. A friend came to his aid from within the bar. Wai Sun was cut up and bruised but was not seriously injured in the brawl. On May 4, 1965, Clarice was honored as Hawaii's 1965 Mother of the year with a reception at Washington Place. The Rev. Abraham K. Akaka, pastor of Kawaiahao Church, praised the role of motherhood in society. "The most precious blessing and gift of God to any person and society, to any child and community is a good and loving and faithful mother." He said. "And with such a mother as you, Mrs. Jeong, and with such a family as you have raised, our community and State and nation are secure. For your kind of love is most like God's love."

Bing Loy, 650 Keawe St. was born in 1909 and died at 2:40 p.m. Friday at Queen's Hospital on October 16, 1940. He was 31 years, 2 months, and 10 days old. He was a truck driver for the Wing Wo Laundry Company. His wife was Jung Shee.

Kam Han was born on October 15, 1894 and died on 27, 1991(97) in Honolulu, HI. She married Sik Kong Chun in 1909. He was born on February 2, 1874 in Canton, China and died on September 30, 1951 in Honolulu. His occupation in 1927 in Hilo, HI was at Tong Wo Restaurant.

Gum Yuk (Ah Yuk), was born on August 2, 1899 and died on December 14 1989 in Kapaa, Kauai. She was adopted by the Kong Pui family in 1904 and lived in Kauai. Pui was born about 1862 in China and Chun Shee was born on October 16, 1882 in Hong Kong and died on March 14, 1978. Ah Yuk married Yin Kong Chu. He was born on May 16, 1875 in Canton, China and died on June 1, 1950 in Kapaa, Kauai. They were married on June 23, 1915.

The second set of twins, Mew Hou and Mew Yung, were born on May 23, 1903 in Honolulu and raised by another family. Mew Yung (Helen Au) married Gee Chung Wong and her adopted parents were Hi Au and Yim See (Wong) Au. Gee Chung was born October 21, 1896 in Honolulu and died at his residence on 1220 N. Vineyard St. on Friday, June 2, 1961 at 3:00 A.M. He was a building construction carpenter at Pacific Naval Air Base in Pearl Harbor. Helen was the mother of Margaret, James Kun(Koon) Sun (Jimmy), Edwin, Agnes, and Irene. Jimmy was my first date. He and Clifford were classmates at Farrington High School. Jimmy was born on October 29, 1923 and passed away on January 10, 2007. He married Annie Gum Nin Lum (1926-1998). On September 1937, Helen had taken a permit for $2600 for a one-story residence at 1232 Vineyard St. She passed away on August 17, 1979 in Honolulu.

Jun Hou, also called Alice, was the youngest aunty. She was born on October 08, 1905 and married Kui Sam Fong, who ran a jewelry store on Hotel Street during the 1950's. They lived at 3071 Wailani Road. Alice passed away on June 26, 1949 at 2:30 P.M. in Queens Hospital. S.M., and Mae S.M.

My brothers were Norman Wing Git, Wing Hoon, Wing(unknown), Raymond Wing Cheong,and Richard Wing Soon. My sisters were Koon Suan and Mary Koon Yong.

Norman (Chick) Wing Git was born on Friday October 8, 1915 in Honolulu, HI and died on August 4, 1997 in Pauoa, Honolulu. He married Mayrose Kaikainahaole on May 1, 1948. She was born on May 4, 1924 in Honolulu, HI and died on December 15, 2006 in Pauoa, Honolulu.

Wing Hoon was born about 1917 in Honolulu and died on Monday March 20, 1922 from diphtheria.

Wing (unknown) was born in 1919 in Honolulu and died in infancy.

Raymond Wing Cheong was born on Monday July 4, 1921 in Honolulu, HI and died on December 22, 1998.

Richard (Bolo) Wing Soon was born on Friday October 26, 1923 in Honolulu, HI and died on August 23, 1989 in Honolulu. He was married to Betty Lou "Lani" Nalanieha Kaikainahaole, who is Mayrose's sister. Lani was born about 1935 in Honolulu, HI and died Monday February 8, 1982.

Koon Suan was born on Thursday January 21, 1926 in Honolulu, HI and died about 1931 in Honolulu.

Mary Koon Yong was born on Sunday March 9, 1930 in Honolulu, HI and married Donald Jay on March 1, 1951. He was born on February 12, 1923 and died November 13, 2000.

I was born on Monday February 27, 1928 at 07:00 p.m. in Honolulu, HI and married Clifford Kwei Chong Wong, a welder at Pearl Harbor Naval Shipyard, on March 21, 1948. Clifford flew alone to San Francisco in May 1958 to look for work and a place to stay. He found work as a welder and transferred to Hunter's Point Naval Shipyard. On August 1958, he returned back to Honolulu and all 6 of us boarded a plane together to San Francisco. We had used up most of our savings for the trip. Wesley was 2-1/2 years old at the time and I carried him in a blanket to pass him off as under 2 years.

We moved into a low-income housing project at 64 Hilltop Drive. Dennis, Kathleen, and Debbie were enrolled at All Hollow's Catholic School. The following year, we had to move because Cliff's income was above the maximum limit. We then moved to an upstairs duplex flat at 283 Carl Street. Six months later, a fire broke out in the kitchen above the stove in the exhaust vent and we had to evacuate.

We stayed with Bill and Lucille Yuen at 2110 Boca Raton Street in Hayward. Bill was a welder and pipe fitter and worked with Cliff at Pearl Harbor and Hunter's Point Naval Shipyards. After several months of the kitchen fire renovation, we weren't allowed to come back to the apartment. The landlord didn't want us back. He blamed us for the fire. We purchased a 3 bedroom,2 bath house at 27098 St. Francis Avenue for $17,999 in 1960. The house was built in 1958 and sold for $15,999. Mr. and Mrs. Joe Texeira had to sell the house due to a divorce. When Renee and Linda were born, we had 4 girls in a room 12 feet by 12 feet. With the help from a friend, we extended the bedroom another 12 feet into the backyard. The room was now 12 feet by 24 feet and there was room for 4 beds. After Wesley was born, we couldn't afford private school for the children and they were enrolled in public school.

When Hunter's Point Naval Shipyard closed down, Cliff worked at Todd's Naval Shipyard in Alameda until his early retirement at the age of 55. Clifford was given a retirement plaque for 38 years and 8 months of Federal Government Service. He was born on Saturday October 6, 1923 in Honolulu, HI and died Tuesday morning at our home at 27098 St. Francis Avenue, Hayward on January 29, 1991. Cliff couldn't sleep the night before and kept tossing and turning. He had stomach pain and got up at midnight to use the toilet. After sitting down for a while, he couldn't move his bowels. He went back to bed. Cliff did not like to go to the hospital or see a doctor. I woke up at 07:00 a.m. and checked on him. His body felt cold; I shook and kept shaking him but he didn't wake up, so, I called my son, Dennis, around 07:30 to come over quickly. Dennis tried to wake Cliff up but was unable. He called 911 and the first responders came over moments later. They entered the house and went straight to the bedroom. It didn't take long to determine that he was dead. His passing was called at 08:15. We were told that he died early morning in his sleep. The coroner reported that the cause of death was cardiac insufficiency due to coronary atherosclerosis.

Cliff was buried in an above ground mausoleum crypt at Chapel of the Chimes in Hayward. I asked the funeral home director to request a military funeral honors ceremony. There was a team of 8 with a non-commissioned officer in charge of the firing detail of 7 honor guards performing the 3 rifle volleys for a 21-gun salute. After the folding of the flag and the sounding of taps, I was presented with the flag and these words: "Please accept this flag as a symbol of our appreciation for your loved one's honorable and faithful service."

Fast forward to Sunday July 20, 2014; I was at Parkmont Care facility in Fremont when my body started shutting down. I was transported in an ambulance to nearby Washington Hospital which was a half mile down the street but I coded and passed away before the ambulance arrived. My daughter, Kathy, had just visited me the weekend before and sensed my declining condition and non-responsiveness.

We had 6 children: 2 sons, Dennis Wai Chung and Wesley Wai Hong; and 4 daughters, Kathleen Mew Lung, Deborah Sau Lung, Renee Ngit Lung, and Linda Joyce Yuke Lung. Our 12 grandchildren were Erica Joy Cobey, twins Clifford Dale and Kenneth Michael Weise, Joseph Michael Vernon, Daniel Wong, Brianne Elizabeth Vernon, Zarek Steven Sen Wong, Mayah Wong, Leanna Marie Carvallyo, Antoine Keoni Nasario, Kayin Tor Nohea Wong, and David Alexander Vernon. I had 14 grandchildren and 10 great grandchildren and saw all my grandchildren graduate from high school.

I am now at peace and joined by Cliff and Debbie.

My philosophy of life

As I grew up, I was by myself. I had a job to do. My father told me that I will be a lucky girl. How lucky? I don't know. My father was very particular. I try to train my children to be particular when they get their own home. That's what I live for. I would come home, and I do my chores. I help my father do the cooking. I had to cook, learn to cook. So, I made lots of soup. I learn from my aunty too. Two of my aunties were kind of staying with my mother. My mother had a home that my aunties all would come over, even my younger aunty was raised by my father before she got married.

I do love all my children. You know that you guys going to amount to something, but I cannot help no more already. I try to help all you guys get a car and get house payment, the beginning payment. I don't have a computer. I just have my TV. Whoever is gifted? I'm gifted in a way, but who I'm going to give it to my children. So, it's a surprise to me. I try to see. I educate myself. I learned to prepare certain things.

"My Journey"

My journey is just beginning,
Continuing,
With no ending.

Searching for a meaning,
Reasoning,
With an understanding.

I reach out to you assisting,
Comforting,
With care providing.

Embracing each day smiling,
Never ending,
With a new beginning.

Dennis W. C. Wong
April 24, 2002

Glossary

Goong Goong – grandfather (Cantonese)

imu – Hawaiian underground oven (Hawaiian)

iron shift – pressing eliminates lifting and placing the iron onto the fabric instead of pushing and shifting the fabric underneath the weight of the iron

lau lau - native Hawaiian entrée made from pork shoulder, seasoned with Hawaiian sea salt, wrapped in luau (taro) leaves, then ti leaves, and steamed, sometimes with a little bit of salted butterfish;

Lung – beautiful (Cantonese)
        Kathleen Mew Lung (beautiful beauty)
        Deborah Sau Lung (adorned beauty)
        Renee Ngit Lung (beautiful moon)
        Linda Joyce Yuke Lung (beautiful jade)

mangle – a rotating padded drum which revolves against a heating element which can be stationary or it can also be a rotating drum. Laundry is fed into the turning mangle and emerges flat and pressed on the other side.

ono – delicious (Hawaiian)

poke – sushi -grade Ahi tuna, round onion, julienne cut, chopped green onions, ogo seaweed

pau – finish or done (Hawaiian)

www.ingramcontent.com/pod-product-compliance
Lightning Source LLC
LaVergne TN
LVHW070437080526
838202LV00038B/2839